PLASTIC RICHES

How to Get Out of Debt and Build Wealth Using Credit Cards

TABLE OF CONTENTS

INTRODUCTION	4
Credit Cards are Not Evil	4
Discipline is Key	6
CHAPTER ONE: PROMOTIONAL GOLD	**9**
Ooh...shiny! Method	9
Gift Card Method	14
Bonus Points Method	17
Statement Credit Method	21
CHAPTER TWO: CONTINUAL PROMOTIONS	**27**
Points Method	27
Cash-Back Method	29
Merchant Discounts	32
Referrals	35
Balance Transfers	36
Third Party Companies	41
CHAPTER THREE: USING 0% APR TO ITS MAXIMUM POTENTIAL	**47**
Pay off Debt	47
Make Purchases and Invest	50
Make a Balance Transfer and Invest	52
CHAPTER FOUR: THE GIFT THAT KEEPS ON GIVING	**63**
Protection Against Fraud	63

Insurance Protection	66
Travel Insurance	66
Ease of Records	66

CHAPTER FIVE: IMPROVING YOUR CREDIT SCORE	**69**

Monitor Your Score	70
Manage Your Credit Cards	73
Sign Up for a Secure Credit Card	78
Pay Your Bills and Negotiate	78
Become an Authorized User	86
Consider Ways to Earn More or Spend Less	87

CHAPTER SIX: BUILDING WEALTH AND INVESTING FOR GROWTH	**89**

Build Your Wealth	89
Mind Your Own Business	92
Educate Yourself	93
Do Your Homework	95
Make Money … Don't Lose It!	96
Build Your Buffer Zones	97
Use Those Credit Cards!	97
Face Your Obstacles	99
Explore a Possibility	100

CONCLUSION	**104**

INTRODUCTION

Have you ever had a great idea on how to make money but didn't follow through? Maybe an invention popped into your head, or you saw a great buy that you knew you could purchase and resell for more. What stopped you from pulling the trigger? While there could be many answers to this question, I would like to address the one I feel anyone can overcome: money.

When you have a great idea but find yourself saying, "Yeah, but I don't have the money," you miss an opportunity. You let a great deal pass you by and it lands in the hands of someone who does have the money. While another opportunity may arise, the one that passed by may never come your way again.

This book will teach you a way to never say "I don't have the money" ever again. That way is *credit cards*.

Credit Cards are Not Evil

The first thing people hear when they find themselves in debt and falling further behind is to cut up all their credit cards. Many people even say to never apply for a credit card.

This, of course, can be very good advice. If someone doesn't have the knowledge and discipline, credit cards can very easily become the enemy. It happens to the best of us. That shiny new toy on the showroom floor. "I don't have the money now, but the payments are so manageable with that low-interest credit card I just got!"

The truth of the matter is, marketing has gotten so good, people find themselves buying things they don't need, or want, all the time. I was stopped at a mall kiosk once, and before I knew it, I spent over $200 for a machine that, I not only didn't need, it only worked once and then broke. Of course, the return policy was "no returns." Now I walk along the edges of the malls so that I don't succumb to my own impulses. Now impulse buying can be silly and relatively unharmful if you have plenty of money in the bank. It's when we pull out the plastic that it can get bad. Low interest rates can jump at the end of a promotional period, and someone is suddenly stuck with a minimum payment that doubles or even triples.

Credit cards can easily become the monsters in our wallets. But they don't have to be. What if, instead of a monster, credit cards could be the fairy godmother to your dreams? Like most fairy tales, the story of credit cards can be seen from more than one point of view. If used correctly, credit cards can make your financial dreams come true.

Credit cards themselves are neutral. It's how you use them that makes them a force for good or evil. In fact, credit cards, when used correctly, not only can save you money but can make you money and be your ticket to building wealth. My goal is to share my story with you. Credit cards became my helping angels. And they are a great source of money that anyone can tap into. I am here to teach you how to use credit cards strategically so you can build your own wealth.

Discipline is Key

Before I get into teaching you how to mine your own plastic gold, I must talk about discipline. You will need discipline to be successful in this program.

First, you will need the discipline to have self-control. I am not an expert on self-control by any means, especially if I'm walking by a dessert case. But when it comes to the strategies I teach in this book, self-control is essential for you to walk the path of the plastic warrior. You don't have to be perfect, but you do need the ability to tell yourself *no*.

Finding yourself with $30,000 of credit card debt when you only stopped at the store to buy milk could cost you years of effort. If you're the type of person that buys every shiny new toy you see just because Mastercard says you can, then your first order of business is to develop a plan to gain self-control. As the old saying goes, "One 'aw, shit' wipes out a thousand 'attaboys'."

This is a strategy that also requires discipline to put in the work. It's not hard work, but it HAS to be done. Keeping track of your budget —which includes your incoming money, your outgoing expenses, your credit limits, your payments, etc.—requires that you are diligent in tracking every aspect of your finances.

When flying a plane, being off by one degree can leave you hundreds of miles from your destination. Likewise forgetting payments, exceeding your limits, or not planning for all your expenses will cause you to miss the mark of financial success. If you currently lack the discipline to keep track of your spending, start small. Keep track of one card diligently and carefully. When you have that down, get another. As you get the hang of it, it will become easier and easier to add to the stack. Like learning to juggle, you start with one ball and work your way up from there. With a little practice, you will find yourself juggling ten credit cards or more with very little extra effort. You can even add in a flaming torch or two.

Last but not least, you will need the discipline to be patient. My plan is a long-term strategy. It takes time to build credit, learn the ins and outs of promotions, and find your niche in the investing world. Things will start out slow, but over time they will gain momentum. At some point, the snowball becomes an avalanche in your favor. With the discipline to have self-control, do the work, and be patient, anyone can find the path that will allow them to finance their dreams.

CHAPTER ONE: PROMOTIONAL GOLD

I'm sure you know that credit cards offer promotions. This is the draw to get you to sign up for a card when you weren't looking for one. Credit card companies offer everything from "no interest" for a set period to "cash in your pocket."

There are two kinds of promotions: one-time offers given to you when you first sign up for a card and promotions or "benefits" that are continuous or can be used more than once. Understanding these promotions is the first step in using credit cards to build wealth. They are the backbone of getting the most out of credit cards.

Let's start with one-time promotions. These are single-use opportunities. In order to take advantage of them multiple times, you would have to open multiple accounts, but it can still be worth the benefits!

Ooh...shiny! Method

One way companies attract you to their cards is by offering exciting one-time rewards in what I call the *ooh...shiny!* tactic. These days the *ooh...shiny!* method is a lot like CDs. You can still find them, but for the most part they have been replaced by their more technologically advanced successors—digital downloads. However, when you do run across an *ooh...shiny!* method being used for credit cards, it is okay to investigate the offer. I still use CDs in my car, after all.

The idea behind this method is to have something tangible to draw people in. Since a lot of people are visual, having something that they can see and touch before they ever even lift a pen helps drive many people to the table who would not otherwise have applied for a credit card. For instance, you might walk into Costco and see someone standing by a table loaded with duffle bags, asking if you have a Costco credit card yet. If you answer "no," then you are asked to fill out an application, and for your trouble, you get a new duffle bag with COSTCO written on the side in big red letters. Now you might not like the big red letters, but if you need a duffle bag to go with your new gym membership (because it is January and this is the year you are going to lose all that weight), then at least it is free.

Picture this. You walk into a store and pass a table with a large stack of small carry-on luggage behind it. Guardian of this stack of luggage is a representative that greets you with a smile. "Hello! Would you like a free piece of luggage?" Free has always been your favorite price, so you walk over to investigate. Now that you are at the table, it is the representative's job to get you emotionally involved. "If you could travel anywhere in the world, where would you go?" they ask. There's no room for a simple "yes" or "no," and it doesn't matter what location you say, because the representative is ready with a response. "Well, all you need to do to get there is apply for this card. You only need to make a small monthly payment to have the vacation of your dreams. We will even give you this carry-on luggage free of charge to help send you on your way. Doesn't that sound wonderful?"

It does sound wonderful. Sitting on a beach, sun warming your skin while sipping your favorite drink. I won't need to save for years, and I don't even need to buy a carry-on bag for the flight. You sign up, awkwardly put your new luggage in your cart, and wish you had signed up on the way *out* of the store.

Of course, most of us are used to this trick. That's why we say, "no thanks," keep our heads down, and keep walking. Even if we went in the store to buy a carry-on bag for an upcoming flight, we still say no. We walk to the appropriate aisle and pay money for something that someone has offered for free. If the luggage costs $25, you now are out that money and it cannot be used somewhere else. However, if you took five minutes to fill out the application, you could have owned the carry-on bag AND had $25 to spend elsewhere. Now imagine if you could replicate those savings and earn $300 an hour!

Most people would jump at a job that pays that well, but they miss those same opportunities to SAVE that well.

You might be saying, "well, what if I wasn't there to buy luggage?" While that may be true, I am sure you buy gifts for people, especially around the holidays. How much do you spend on them? What if someone you know needed luggage? What if you had been filling out credit card applications all year round?

My wife follows this principle in her regular shopping. This used to drive me crazy because we were always spending money on gifts with no person or event in mind. Then one Christmas years ago we were short on money. I told my wife all we would be able to afford was cards for everyone. Smiling, she guided me over to a cabinet in a spare room. She opened the doors, and lo and behold, there were items she had been stocking up on for years. Two-for-one books, Christmas decorations bought in January, board games never opened. She even had boxes of holiday cards with envelopes and wrapping paper that she had bought at 75% off. We were able to give everyone we knew a gift without even cracking open my wallet. On that day, I saw the value of the *ooh...shiny!*

A bonus to this promotional tactic is that even if you don't get approved, there is no penalty for taking the gift. Likewise, if you cancel the card, you still get to keep the gift. While this is one of the least profitable ways to make money on credit cards, it has saved me hundreds of dollars over the years. As long as you have the discipline to take the luggage and not purchase the vacation, or something else you did not plan on buying, this method can save anyone money, anytime it should appear.

My First Time

I remember the very first time I got a credit card. I was eighteen and in the middle of basic training for the United States Army. Back then, cell phones were rare, and payphones were still common. I did not have a cell phone, but someone told me I could get a free 250-minute phone card if I applied for an AAFES credit card. At the time, I didn't care that the credit card could only be used at specific stores that are only found on military establishments. What I did care about was a phone card that would save me $50 if I was willing to take a few minutes of my time.

I didn't realize it at the time, but this was classic *ooh...shiny!* The funny thing is that I never received a copy of the card, yet two years later, when I applied for a loan, I had great credit because I had a two-year-old credit card that I'd never been late paying. (Not hard to never be late when you have not ever used the card!) That good credit allowed me to qualify for the loan, all because of the first *ooh...shiny!* that caught my fancy.

Gift Card Method

One step up from the *ooh...shiny!* promotion is the gift card promotion. This is frequently used by online retailers. These days, shopping for anything can be done not only in the comfort of your own home, but also in the comfort of your underwear. Shopping online has grown so much over the last two decades that even groceries are now delivered to your door. Gone are the days where you had to pick out your own produce. Now, if you bite into a bad grape, you can blame someone else. Of course, almost all major stores have their own website and, with it, their own credit card.

I am sure everyone that has shopped online has been met with "Would you like a free $XX gift card today?" It is a question that could pay to say *yes* to. Gift cards are as good as cash. Why would you not want free cash? All you must do is sign up for the credit card. However, in this digital age, the gift card is often just a code for the next time you shop on that site. It can also often be applied to the purchase you are there to make in the first place. This works out great for the online store. Like the *ooh...shiny!* method, you get drawn in with the idea of an immediate freebie. But unlike *ooh...shiny!,* the store doesn't have to choose and buy a product, ship it, store it, hire someone to hand it out, or worry about whether or not people want that particular item. Yet, they still entice people to apply for the credit card. Another benefit for the retailer is that if you don't get approved, they don't give you the gift card and they are out nothing. The benefit for you, if you do get approved, is the money you saved from the gift card. Additionally, if you get approved instantly and can apply the card to your current shopping experience, then you get what you were going to buy anyway at a cheaper price. It feels great to check out and buy my $55 item for $5.

But what if you don't get approved right away? If you don't get approved at all, then you need to work on improving your credit score. (Check out the chapter of this book which explains how to do that.) If you get approved, but not instantly—which can happen for many reasons—then you will still get the gift card later and still save money. That savings makes it worth your time to apply for the card.

I know there are some naysayers out there claiming, "but this was a one-time thing. I am never going to buy at this store again." That could be very true. I have often shopped at stores that I have never shopped at again. The great thing about gift cards these days is even though they "have no cash value," they really do. Most gift cards can be sold for cash. The amount of cash may only be half of the value of the gift card, but if you had no other use for it, this is still a great trade and a viable way to make money on the gift-card method.

Most gift cards handed out for credit card applications range from $25–$50. Say you apply for a card and are given a $25 gift card for the five minutes it takes you to apply. You can accept the gift card, then go to a website that buys gift cards and spend five minutes selling it to them. They pay you $12.50 for your card. This means you received $12.50 for your ten minutes of time. If you did that for a living, you would be earning $75 an hour. Of course, you make more by using the gift card for things you need, but what if you need cash? What if you were trying to buy a house and needed money for a down payment?

This method of making money does depend on your credit and ability to be approved for credit cards. Thus, it's not something you can do every day. You could, however, get an extra $50–$100 a month reasonably with this method.

Getting even an extra $50 a month with gift cards can really help speed things up. For instance, imagine you were saving for a down payment on a home, and you needed $12,000. If you could put away $100 a month of your own money into savings (which is no small feat for a lot of people), it would take you 12 years to save up the money you need to buy a home. If you could save an extra $50 each month by using the gift card method, you would then only need to save for six years, eight months. That is five years, four months sooner that you would get to live in your own home.

I usually use this method as a savings tool. When I get a gift card, I use it to buy something I need already, then take the money I would have spent on that item and put it into savings for a larger purchase. You might think of the gift-card method as a huge time commitment of surfing the web to find these opportunities, but if you take advantage of the offers when they pop up, you could casually save hundreds of dollars a year doing what you were already doing, without using any extra time.

Bonus Points Method

Many credit cards allow you to accrue points and/or "miles" based on what you spend. I'll talk about these types of points in a later section. The points I am talking about now are the points you get when you first sign up for a card. These are called "bonus" points. Typically, if you spend a certain amount of money within a specified amount of time, you earn bonus points—typically between 25,000 and 50,000 points. That usually translates into $250–$500 for this method.

The downside to the bonus points is that you are often limited on how or where you can use the points. Because of this, I suggest that before you sign up for a card with the expectation of earning points toward a goal, make sure you check into what the points can actually be redeemed for. It would suck to want to spend them on a flight to Hawaii only to find out they can only be redeemed for hotel stays.

However, most limitations still allow you to get some amazing rewards. Some of the typical items you can redeem points for are airline flights (which is why they are sometimes called "miles"), hotel stays, or restaurant certificates.

While some of you may not travel much, this method could still help save money. Why not take your spouse out for an anniversary getaway to a local hotel paid for by points? Not only can you save money by not buying a traditional gift, this is also a great way to earn "double points" with your spouse. Or you could fly to see family that you would not normally be able to afford to see. You will often find these opportunities around the holidays. Merry Christmas anyone?

While bonus points can be very profitable, this method does require the most work. First, you must earn the points. After you have earned them, you must redeem them. Redeeming points usually requires you to go online to the card's website or call the card's customer service number and shop for what you want to spend your points on. Then finally, you spend the points.

Don't let this seemingly long sequence of steps stop you, though. Being able to save a large chunk of money at one time can be worth all the planning and effort.

> **The Free Vacation**
>
> The points method has been a great success for me. Remember, sometimes points are counted in miles. One fall, I decided I wanted to attend Gencon the following summer in Indianapolis. Gencon is a gaming convention. (Yes, I am a nerd! I am writing a book about credit cards after all!) In fact, Gencon is known as "The Biggest Four Days in Gaming." The total cost of the trip was going to be about $1,200.
>
> The problem was that my budget did not allow for this trip. My wife and I had previously agreed that I would only attend if I could do so for free. I was in possession of a free-entry ticket, but I needed to cover the cost of hotel, airfare, and food.

I had won a PlayStation 4 (PS4) at an event earlier in the year, so I started off by trading the PS4 for some items, which I turned around and sold to a friend. That cash covered my hotel cost.

When it came to food, I knew it would not be a big expense, and I could get away with $25 a day for food. That left airfare, which at the time ran about $450. I knew I could talk my wife into letting me spend $100 on food, but a $450 plane ticket was out of the question.

So how did I get the money? My good friend American Express paid for it. I had recently received an offer from American Express that said if I spent $500 within three months, the company would reimburse me up to $500 for airline tickets. With that good news, I applied for the card, got it in the mail, and began using it for gas and groceries. I bought my plane ticket with that card as well, and a few months later, I headed off for the biggest four days in gaming, with food as my only out-of-pocket expense. Thank you, American Express!

Statement Credit Method

Have you ever had anyone pick up a tab for you? It's happened to me a couple of times, and it is a great feeling. That is why the next method is one of my favorites. Many cards offer a statement credit as a one-time enticement for signing up for their credit card. What does this mean? They will pay a portion of your bill for you.

The mechanics of earning this reward is similar to the bonus points method. After you spend a certain dollar amount—typically between $500 and $1000—you receive a credit, most commonly between $100 and $200. However, unlike the points method, it requires no extra work. The credit shows up on your statement without you needing to do a thing. Say you are required to spend $500 to receive a $100 credit. This means that when you spend $500 on the card, you only owe $400 back. It is straight-up cash in the bank. No need to redeem points in any way.

With this method, it's important that you have the self-discipline (we talked about this before!) to only spend on what you really need and had planned for in the first place. If you spend more, just to receive your statement credit, you are still spending more. Remember, the goal is to **build wealth**. With any of these methods, you want to make sure you are only buying items you had planned to buy in the first place, and that you can pay the card off completely each time period, so you are not losing what you have gained by paying interest.

I have seen cards offer as much as $200 in credit for spending only $500 on the card. That is a 40% discount! Many utilities allow the use of credit cards to pay the cost for their service. If you have a phone or cable bill that allows payment by credit card, using one that gives you a statement credit could allow you to reach the required spending amount quickly without the temptation of having a plastic money bag in a store. What would you do with the extra money if all your bills were suddenly reduced by 40% less?

> **My Plastic Raise**
>
> I have never found a single person who would turn down a raise at work. I have, however, met several people that have worked for years without such a benefit. I consider statement credits from credit cards as my raise.
>
> I have gotten to the point where I almost only apply for cards that offer a statement credit. With my current money expenses, I cover the minimum requirement for one card per month. To maximize this benefit, I apply for cards periodically to keep my credit from dropping from too many inquiries. I have come to average around $2,000 a year in statement credits. If I was to break this down

monthly, that would be the equivalent to a $167 a month raise. Don't wait for your boss to call you into his office. Go to your mailbox and start collecting your own plastic raise.

Mailbox Madness

I wanted to share some actual offers I received in my mailbox while writing this book:

Bank of America Business Advantage Cash Rewards MasterCard:

- No annual fee (almost always a must if you ask me)
- 1% to 3% cash back on purchases
- $200 statement credit if you spend $500 in the first 60 days
- 0% APR on purchases for 9 billing cycles

US Bank American Express

- No annual fee
- 1.5% cash back on all purchases
- $150 Statement credit after spending $500 in the first 90 days
- 0% APR for 15 billing Cycles

USAA Visa Card (USAA works with military veterans)

- No annual fee

- 0% APR for 12 months on balance transfers (the transfer fee is 3% or $200, whichever is lower)

- 2500 bonus rewards points

Wells Fargo Platinum Visa

- No annual fee

- 0% APR on purchases and balance transfers for 15 months

Chase Slate

- 0% APR balance transfer for 12 months (I received the money in a check, so I could deposit the money into my own back account to use for anything I wanted)

Capital One

- No annual fee

- Unlimited 1.5% cash back on all purchases

- $200 Statement credit when you spend $1,000 in 90 days

- 0% APR on purchases and balance transfers for 15 months

KeyBank Mastercard

- No annual fee

- $200 deposited into KeyBank savings account—no purchase is necessary, but you would need a KeyBank savings account

- 0% APR on purchases and balance transfers for 15 months

Alaska Mileage Plan Visa (offer from Bank of America)

- $50 annual fee (boo!)

- Buy one/get one for your first plane ticket—this could be as much as $500

- Free companion fare every year (up to $121)

- 30,000 bonus miles after spending $1,000 in 90 days

- Free checked bags when you fly

Citi Diamond Card

- 0% APR Balance transfer for 12 months (receivable in a check so I could deposit money directly into my bank account)

- 0% APR on purchases for 6 months

American Express

- No annual fee

- 15,000 bonus points (valued at $150) after spending $1,000 in 90 days.

- 0% APR on purchases and balance transfers for 15 months

- Points earned with every purchase.

In these offers alone there is $950 in statement credits, 47,500 bonus points, and free airfare. There is also the potential of years of free interest. Maybe you should go check your mailbox.

The methods I have spoken on so far are a one-time thing. Occasionally you get an extra gift card or some bonus points, but I would not expect it. These promotions are designed to draw you in. Once you are hooked, you stop getting free samples. Thus, the next chapter will focus on credit card benefits that stick around the entire time you own the card. The savings you get through them are significantly less than the sign-up promotions, but they can reduce your overall cost of living, thus helping you save money in the long run.

CHAPTER TWO: CONTINUAL PROMOTIONS

Now that we've discussed the initial promotional benefits, it's time to delve into continual promotions you might receive.

Before I begin, I must reiterate what I've said before. **Properly using credit cards to build wealth relies on your ability to be disciplined.** You must limit yourself to only purchasing items that you could otherwise buy with cash, debit card, or check. If you buy more than you can afford, you will not be able to pay off the credit card each month. This results in high interest, fees, and a subsequent loss of savings through the plastic shackles you have created for yourself. On the other hand, if you can use credit cards wisely, you may find yourself with plastic wings carrying you to a brighter financial future.

Points Method

This promotion is similar to the bonus points method previously mentioned, except now you earn points only as you spend with your credit card. After you accrue enough points, you can redeem those points for a reward. The rewards are so varied that it would take its own book just to cover them. However, the rewards themselves are not what is important (as long as the reward is something that you would have been willing to spend money on in the first place). What is important is the value of each point. Typically, the average ratio is one point to $1. The value is determined by dividing the value of the reward by the number of points needed to redeem that reward.

As an example, 2,500 points typically can get you a $25 gift card. $25/2,500 = .01 or 1%.

It is not uncommon to only get 0.5% or even 0.25% on the money you spent. This a low return on your spending and requires you to spend time shopping for the reward.

Often companies have tiers for their points and there is no way to take advantage of a partial reward. For example, having 2,000 points does not allow you to get a $20 gift card. You must comply with whatever rules and points the company sets. Unless you use the card forever or cancel it at the exact time you have a redeemable number of points, you will lose points and reduce the effective value of the point method.

Because of these drawbacks, I think this is the least effective benefit and use of credit cards. I only recommend it because if all other permanent reward programs are unavailable to you or the rewards are specific enough to you that the overall value is increased, the point method still allows you to take advantage of some savings until you find a card that offers a better deal.

Cash-Back Method

While many companies started with the points method mentioned above, the majority now offer a cash-back reward as well.

The basic idea between both these programs is the same: a percentage discount on everything you purchase, based on their offered reward percentage. However, the cash-back method offers increased benefits and less drawbacks.

The basic idea of the cash-back method is that for every dollar you spend, you get 1% back in cash at a later date. You could receive a check for the 1%, or you could receive the 1% in the form of a refund applied to your card balance. I have also seen these cash-back rewards paid as a prepaid Visa card. While 1% might not seem like much, you must remember that as long as you only purchase those items you were going to buy anyway, you're effectively buying everything for less. If you then have the discipline to take that savings and use it to pay off debt early or to invest, it will help free you from debt and consequently build wealth.

Unlike the point method, the cash-back method usually has no minimums. This means if you only spend $10 you will still receive $.10 as a reward. You will never have to reach some limit of spending to take advantage of the benefit. If you spend $100 or $10,000 you still get the same reward: 1% cash back.

Another benefit this has over points is there is no limitation on how you use your reward. You can spend cash on whatever you want. Instead of getting a $25 gift card to Olive Garden, the only restaurant that may be available to redeem your points, you can just take your $25 cash and eat wherever you want.

There are even more effective ways to use the cash-back method if your credit card offers percentages on categories of purchases (think meals, entertainment, travel, etc.) For instance, one card may let you choose between ground transportation, gyms and fitness, or restaurants. If you have the discipline to calculate which budget category you spend the most on and then find a card that will allow you 5% back for items purchased in that category, you could receive a higher percentage of cash back.

Using these calculations, myself, I was able to bring my total average of cash-back reward to about 2.1% on a card that offered from 1% to 5%, depending on the category of spending.

Some people save more by having multiple cards! They make sure that none of the categories overlap and then use the appropriate card for appropriate purchases. This is great for those of you who love spreadsheets and have a large amount of discipline to keep track of it all. For the rest of us, my recommendation is to find a card that will give you the maximum cash back on what you spend and use it for all your purchases. This will give you the benefit of using a credit card to earn cash back without spending the time equivalent of a part-time job in order to keep track of all your purchases.

Remember though, the idea behind receiving cash back is not to spend more. It is to take that savings and either pay off debt that's not helping you make money or invest it to help create wealth.

> **My Plastic Tax Return**
>
> I have been using cash back cards for years. My current cash back card pays you the reward in the form of a check every year. Not only does this allow me to see precisely how much I did save, it also gives me a large lump sum that can easily be used to pay off a debt or invest.
>
> Currently, this cash back check ranges from $1,000 to $2,000 a year. Most people already know what it is like to

> get a large check once a year from doing your taxes. We also tend to spend it and then wish for another. Alas, tax season comes but once a year. But with credit cards you can enjoy that tax return check feeling more than once. What would you do with an extra yearly check?

Merchant Discounts

Merchant discounts are a great tool but are somewhat unknown. They come about through contracts made between companies to mutually benefit each other by increasing the likelihood that you will shop with a specific merchant using a specific credit card. The idea behind merchant discounts is that if you use your credit card to shop at a specific business you can get a discount in some way.

The discount amount and method depends on what card you use, what store you shop at, and how the discount is redeemed. Methods include shopping through your credit card's website which links to other store websites, buying gift cards through your credit card's website at a discounted rate, or signing up through the card's website to receive statement credits from specific purchases.

The savings from merchant discounts can be massive. I have seen them range from 3% to 100%. Yes, I said 100%! For instance, you might see an offer where you can spend $10 on Uber and get a $10 statement credit.

For those of you saying, "I bet the places I shop at don't offer these great deals," I would say think again. The variety of places you can shop to receive discounts is quite vast. Your shopping options include restaurants, home improvement stores, department stores, cell phone companies, travel, theaters, and much much more.

And they aren't just small names. You'll find large brand names like Home Depot, Macys, Apple, Expedia, Adidas, GNC, Bath and Body Works, etc. I am confident that because of the vast number of places to save money, anyone can use merchant discount to shop for things they planned on buying anyway and see a change in their financial standing.

Your opportunity's also increase with each new card you get, because you are open to the deals that multiple providers offer. Sometimes, you can even use them to double down. For instance, if you have a credit card that offers gift cards at a discount, you can then shop for sales that allow you to maximize the savings you can receive for your shopping ingenuity.

This method works for many types of people, as well. If you are a fly by the seat of your pants kind of person, you could easily browse the credit card company's site anytime you want to purchase something and see where you can save. Maybe you are the planning type and you have a large project, like a kitchen remodel, on the horizon. What if you found Home Depot gift cards at 10% off? And waited for a 10% off sale in the store? You could easily find yourself saving 10% to 20% on a $50,000 kitchen remodel, thus saving you $5,000 to $10,000. For most of us the difference of $5,000 to $10,000 could be the difference between getting a kitchen remodel and not getting one.

Why doesn't everyone do this? Typically, customers don't know how to find these discounts. Merchant discount details are often placed in the small print of the bill or agreement and most people don't read every word of their bill—much less the agreement they made when they sign up for a card! Credit card websites often bury them in two to four clicks of dropdown menus, making them hard to find unless you are looking for them. Even when someone does find them, it is often hard to figure out exactly how it works. It's no wonder these discounts are missed. That being said, it is more than worth it to do the work to familiarize yourself with your options and explore this vast world of savings.

Referrals

Referrals allow you to make money when you bring someone else to the credit card company as a new client. You make the suggestion, the person applies, and if they are approved you get a referral fee.

Many people are unaware that credit cards offer referrals, but it's a great way to earn a few extra dollars! The cool thing about this plastic portal to cash is that you don't even have to charge against the card or make the payments. That's all on the new user.

Before reading this book, you might have believed that convincing someone to get a credit card would be something you only wished on your enemies. I hope that I've changed your mind a little and you won't feel as if you scammed a friend by putting a plastic "Benjamin" in their wallet, but rather that you've given them the chance to open the door to previously undiscovered benefits.

So how much does this perk get you? I've seen referral fees as high as $100 dollars, so it's not like you need a massive pool of people to pull from with referrals. And, while this might not be a major way of using credit cards to make money for the majority of people reading this book, it can be lucrative for those who are interested. In fact, some people have created websites dedicated to making money solely from referrals for credit cards!

(I admit that I personally have not used this method. I know I am leaving money on the table, but honestly, I often get so carried talking about the great things about credit cards with people, I forget to even consider trying to get a referral. So, in this instance, don't be me! Take the time to help yourself while you are helping others.)

Balance Transfers

Finally, we've reached the most beneficial promotion of all: the 0% APR (Annual Percentage Rate) balance transfer.

I am sure most people have seen offers for this but never realized how effective it can be to help you save money and build wealth. While I have used (and continue to use) all of the methods in this book, the balance transfer promotion is the one that's given me the greatest ability to save and build wealth.

Imagine, you open an offer for a credit card. On the first page you read in big letters: 0% APR for the first 12months. A lot of people think, "Sure 0% for 12 months, but then they jack it up to 30% and I will end up paying four times what I would have."

While this *could* happen, it does not *have* to happen. What if you paid off your balance before twelve months? Then you are effectively getting a loan for free! Remember though, it is not that you can get a loan for free for a year, or even up to two years, it is what you do with it that counts.

The balance transfer promotion can be a one-time thing or a reoccurring benefit. Quite a few cards will offer you a promotional rate when you first sign up for a card, which is great, but it is even better when you have a card that also offers it to you periodically.

So how do you use this effectively? You pay off another type of interest-bearing debt. Or you put the money straight into your bank account and use it to earn other income, virtually for free. (I say virtually, because it is very rare to be able to take advantage of this without paying a fee. The typical fee ranges from two to five percent of the amount you borrow.)

Let's examine this a little further. Let's say that prior to reading this book you got a credit card to a clothing store. You racked up $1,000 and now pay the minimum monthly payment. For ease of this example, let's say your minimum payment is $100, half of which goes to interest and half goes to the principal. That's $50 a month that disappears into thin air. If you were only able to make those minimum payments, it would take you 20 months to hit a zero balance, assuming you never used the card again and you never missed a payment.

When you hit a zero balance, you would have paid $2,000 against your original $1,000 debt.

Now let's say you get a letter from a bank saying they are willing to give you a credit card with a limit of $1,100 (it must be more than the amount owed in order to cover the fee of the transfer). They will let you transfer $1,000 from your new card to the credit card you owe $1,000 on, leaving you with a zero balance on the old card. The cost of this transaction will be 3% or $30, but they promise not to charge you interest for 12 months. You continue to pay $100 a month to the new card, but since that card is not yet charging interest, it only takes you 11 months to pay off the debt, with the last month only being $30, not $100. That means the total cost was $1030, saving you $970 and 13 months of payments. And, since it took less than 12 months to pay it all back, you never have to pay more than the 3% fee.

This is the power of the 0% APR promotions. At first it might not seem wise to trade $1,000 of debt for $1,030, but what matters is the total amount needed to pay off the debt. As you can see in the example, you save far more than the cost.

This method, of course, takes discipline as well. When you first make the balance transfer, your new minimum payment could be $25 a month, making you feel like you are saving $75 a month right off the bat. That is the trap. If you pay only the minimum required instead of the payment you were previously paying, by the end of the zero-interest period you will still have a balance and you will begin paying interest again. The only thing you accomplish is delaying the interest cost.

Now, what if you can't pay off the total amount in the given time period? Perhaps you owe a lot more than $1,000, or the payments you can afford are not high enough to cover the entire debt before the promotion ends.

This is where multiple promotions come in handy.

Perhaps you receive another offer in your mailbox before the first year is over. If you were to transfer the money to a new card that has another 0% APR promotion, it would cost you another 3% fee, but if you can always bounce it back and forth before you begin to pay interest, you effectively reduce your interest rate to 3% per year. It can even be less than that if you find a promotion that will give you 18 or 24 months at 0% interest, instead of 12.

If you could take all the debt you have from credit cards, student loans, car payments, or any other debt and reduce the interest rate to 3% per year—as a one-time fee, not even compounding interest—you could save hundreds, if not thousands of dollars a year, and have debt paid off in less than half the time.

This is the secret of paying off debt with credit cards.

This is also the secret of how to use credit cards to build wealth. As the saying goes, "It takes money, to make money." While I don't believe this is wholly true, it is easier to make money when you already have some. And it is that lack of money that stops a lot of people from pursuing their dreams. The thing to remember is, no one ever said it had to be your own money. Lots of people have heard the phrase "other people's money" or "OPM," but while many people tell you to use OPM, most don't tell you how to get OPM. It is this method of using credit cards that I have found to be the easiest and most accessible way to get OPM.

How often have you been turned down for a loan (auto, home, etc.)? A loan from a bank or other lending institution can be difficult to get. Some loans require a down payment, leaving many to say, "If I had the thousands of dollars for a down payment laying around, I wouldn't need the loan in the first place!" Yet even if you are consistently turned down left and right for bank loans, credit card advertisements still show up in your mailbox almost every day.

Note: even though credit card companies are not as picky as banks, they will still turn you down if you have bad credit. Chapter four will talk about ways to improve your credit score.

Before we get there, let's talk about a little known way to use credit cards to pay even bigger payments. I have yet to see a bank accept Visa for the mortgage payment ... but you'll be surprised at how you can get around it!

Third Party Companies

Third party companies are another tool in the tool belt of the plastic world. While they are not directly a benefit from credit cards, they allow for more versatility in their use.

A third party company accepts a credit card payment and then sends a check out on your behalf to other companies that do not directly accept credit cards. For instance, you could charge a credit card with a third party company and they could send a check to your mortgage provider to cover your mortgage payment.

The benefit for you is that you can now use credit cards to pay bills that don't accept them. The benefit for the third party company is that they charge a fee for the service—which is often 3% (or less) of the amount of money being sent via a check. The fees charged vary and often times the third party companies have promotions that allow you to get the fee reduced.

Now, many of you are probably wondering. If you have the money already and the third party company charges you, why would you ever use a third party company? Sometimes people need to use them. And sometimes the benefit outweighs the charge.

In the first example, let's say you would like to make an investment, you've done your due diligence, but you don't have the time to use the purchase method. Or perhaps the card you want to use to invest is new and won't allow a balance transfer straight to your account. You could use the third party company to be your middle man. They will charge your card and then send the check out in your name to make your investment. Yes, there is a small fee but you don't miss the opportunity.

In the second example, let's say you are offered a card that has a very good promotion, but it requires you spend $5,000 to $10,000 dollars in a short amount of time to take advantage of the promotion.

Most people don't spend $5,000 to $10,000 on everyday expenses in one to three months. This leaves that large opportunity on the table. But with third party companies you can make those large payments (mortgage/rent, automobile, etc.) on items that normally don't take a credit card. This can allow you to fulfill the original promotional terms while still only paying for things you would have paid for in the first place.

Note: There are two things to keep in mind when using third party companies. First, you still need to only use them to purchase items you can afford. Second, make sure the cost of using the company is outweighed by the benefit received. If you can follow these two rules even more doors can be opened using third party companies.

My Plastic Mortgage Payment

I have received many credit card offers that require me to spend as much as $10,000 in three months or less to receive a large statement credit or amount of points. To this day, I rarely spend that much money in the required time unless I am working on a large project at the time.

The first time I received one of these offers I was given the chance to get a $2,000 statement credit if I could spend $10,000 in three months or less. $2,000 was a large enough number that I really wanted to find a way to make it work. $100 to $200 statement credits are great but $2,000 would be amazing. I was well short of spending $10,000 in three months on things that would accept credit cards even if I used this card for absolutely everything I needed to get. Unwilling to give up, I started searching the internet for solutions.

That's when I discovered third party companies. At the time, my mortgage payment was around $2,000 a month. Three months of payments would be $6,000 and with my other charges, I was easily able to reach the $10,000 criteria.

The third party company I used normally charged a 2.5% to send out checks. $6,000 worth of mortgage payments equated to only $150 in fees. And as a first time user of the company, the fee was dropped to 1.5% for the time I needed it, thus reducing my fees down to $90. This left my a net gain $1,910.

In essence, this credit card made one of the three mortgage payments for me. I was never so happy to have a friend made out of plastic!

CHAPTER THREE: USING 0% APR TO ITS MAXIMUM POTENTIAL

Some promotions offer you a 0% APR on purchases as well as balance transfers. Most cards that offer you a 0% APR on balance transfers when you first sign up for the card will also offer that same 0% on purchases made on that card within a certain time frame. The great thing about a 0% APR on purchases is that is does not come with the balance transfer fee that you would have to pay to transfer the debt.

As for the time frame, I have seen everything allowed from purchases made the first month to any purchase made the entire length that the promotional rate is offered. So how do you use a 0% APR promotion on purchases to pay a debt to someone that does not accept credit cards? The answer is *discipline*.

Pay off Debt

One way to use this 0% APR is to use a credit card to buy everyday things that you were already planning on buying, then take the cash you would have used for those everyday things and pay off a debt.

For instance, what if you owed $5,000 dollars on student loans? This is a typical type of debt that you cannot pay off with a credit card. So, in this instance, you use your credit card to buy $5,000 worth of food, gas, clothes, etc., then take the cash you could have used for those items and pay off the student loan.

The average person does not spend $5,000 dollars a month on their expenses, so it may take you a few months to pull off this trick; but since there is no fee to use the card and the interest is zero, it will cost you no extra money to do it. For those of you that fear you can't pay off the $5,000 dollars before the promotion is over, let me put your mind at ease.

A lot of student loans have an interest rate higher than 3%. So after you use this method and your debt is on a credit card, you can use another credit card to do a balance transfer, and only pay that 3% fee.

See! It's all coming together now.

Let's take a look at the numbers to see what exactly you'll be saving:

If your student loan has a 6% interest rate, you'll be paying approximately $300 a year in interest. Let's say you planned to pay off the loan in the next 5 years. That's an extra $1,500 in interest paid out over the life of the loan.

Now let's say you decide to transfer your loan to a credit card and can only find promotions that last 12 months with a 3% fee for a transfer.

The first year you use the 0%-on-purchases method, so the first year you will pay zero extra dollars in interest. Over the next 4 years you pay a 3% fee to transfer it from card to card to avoid high interest rates. That means that you are paying $150 a year for 4 years in fees. The total cost in interest is now $600, which is $900 less to pay off the same debt than it would have taken.

(In actuality, you will save more because as the debt gets paid down you have a lower balance, resulting in a lower transfer fee. Also, the transfer fee is charged up front, so it is fixed, whereas the interest charged on the student loan was compounding.)

The Used Car Salesman

I ran into a used car salesman while writing this book. I asked some questions about his business and found out that he obtains loans to purchase the cars he sells. Each time he purchases a car, he pays a fee based on the cost of car. For instance, any vehicle under $5,000 has a $55 fee to borrow the money needed to purchase said vehicle. The interest is 10% compounded daily (that's right, I said daily). There are other associated fees with using the lending service as well.

I asked if he had any credit cards. He responded that he had one but rarely used it. I spent the next hour explaining how he could possibly save money using credit cards.

I called him back a few weeks later to see how things had gone. He was able to open a credit card with a $15,000 limit. They gave him access checks to go with it. He used an access check to get $12,000 with a 3% fee, costing him $360, and 18 months no interest. This $12,000 has the potential to save him as much as $5,000 to $15,000 over the course of the 18 months by eliminating interest and fees that his earlier process cost him. And this is just the first card he got!

Make Purchases and Invest

Using the 0%-on-purchases promotion for investing works exactly the same way as above. Many investment opportunities will now let you use a credit card, which means you have no extra work other than finding what you want to invest in and then handing them your card. For those that don't accept credit cards, you would still use the card to buy everyday things you would have anyway, but this time instead of spending your cash on a debt that would not accept a credit card, you simply use the money for your investment.

Let's look at an example.

You want to start making money by flipping cars but don't have enough money to purchase the first car. If you usually spend $2,000 cash on bills and necessities each month, you could purchase those items on your credit card, leaving you with the $2,000 cash (the money you did not spend from your source of income) and $2,000 of debt on a credit card with a 0% APR that would have a minimum payment of around $50.

The next month, you could buy a car that cost up to $2,000 for the cost of the car and parts, repair it, and sell it for $3,000. You then pay back the credit card and have $1,000 profit to use on the next deal or help support your life in some other way.

Note: I have never flipped a car in my life. I do know there are limitations on selling them without the proper licensing, depending on the state. But the scenario illustrates that, no matter how you want to make money, credit cards can help get you there.

Without the credit card and its promotion, you would miss out on this deal and not have made the extra $1,000. While this math may be confusing, the important thing to remember is that using the 0%-purchase method can free up cash to use in other places without costing you any extra in fees or interest.

Even if you don't have any debt, you can still use this plastic superpower to raise thousands of dollars of cash, allowing you to go after something that can make you money. This could be buying that food truck you want or starting an online business. Maybe you could even fund a prototype of that new invention you dreamed up!

Make a Balance Transfer and Invest

When you first obtain a credit card, you can typically transfer the balance from another credit card to the new one with the 0% APR promotion. Rarely can you do a balance transfer that gives you cash in hand with a new card. Why?

When the card is new, you don't have an established relationship with the card company. They don't know if you are going to make the payments on time or at all, so they tend to limit how the card is used. Rather than letting you put money into your bank account as cash, they will allow you to use the money to pay off another debt. That way they at least know you no longer owe the other debt, and perhaps you will spend the money you were using to pay the old debt to the new debtor. After some time has passed and you have developed a history, most companies tend to loosen the reins a bit and allow you bigger and better promotions.

What does that promotion look like?

Suppose you have had a card for a couple of years. You made great use of the promotion for opening the account, but the debt has been paid off and you have not used the card for months. Why would you use it? There is no reason to without the great benefit of 0% interest, and this is not your cash-back card, so it sits in a box on your desk. Don't think that the credit card company hasn't noticed. You don't write, you don't call. What are they supposed to think other than you don't find their card as attractive as you used to? Let's face it, 10% interest or more doesn't look good on any card. So, what do they do? They send you a letter. Yes, a letter is a little old fashioned, but they want to grab your attention and what better way than putting something in your hand, so you have to stop and notice it.

When you come across this letter, it stops you for a second because you know you haven't used this card in long time. This can't be a bill, so what is it? You open it up to find two checks, called access checks, with your name on them. There is also a letter from the credit card company:

> Dear Mr. Doe,
>
> We haven't heard from you in a while. Do you want to use our card again? If you do, we'll let you have 0% interest again. At least for a little while.

If you are given this offer, not only do you want to keep that card forever, you should also try to apply for as many cards as the bank or lender will allow. My three current favorites are Citibank, Chase, and Discover.

Because, let's face it, 0% looks good on any card. The offer draws you in, and the checks seem to imply "go out and get yourself something pretty." The principal behind the checks is as follows: if you write them out and cash them, you agree to the terms in the letter sent along with the checks. Usually, you get 12-24 months no interest or low interest—make sure to read the terms—and have to pay a small fee—again make sure to read the terms—and the checks that are cashed will be treated as a balance transfer. It is very easy to pay off debt with a check, but we are talking about getting cash for a possible investment at this point.

So how do you get the cash? After all, checks are great, but cash is king.

What some people don't understand is that the checks you get this way don't have to be written to someone else. That's right, you can write your name on the payee line, take it to your bank and deposit it into your account. Voila! You have just used a credit card balance-transfer promotion to get cash at a 0% interest rate which you may now use on anything you want. You can sometimes do this with no fee, making it entirely free, but don't count on it. Even with a fee, compared to the other ways of getting a loan, this is almost always the cheapest option.

Let's take the car-flipping example used in the 0% APR purchase method and add in a 3% fee because you are now using the balance-transfer method. You still get $2,000 to buy and flip the car, but your profit (if you sell for $3,000) is only $940 because you have a $60 fee.

At first glance this may make the purchase method seem like the better choice. However, the benefit of no fee might be offset by the cost of time. It takes time to build up cash through the purchase method, sometimes a few months. That means any deals that come your way while you are building up cash might have to pass you by. While you make slightly less using a balance transfer, it usually only takes a couple of days for the check too clear, being able to save you a lot of time. Plus, whoever you buy the car from might take checks, leaving you with no lag time at all.

Again, using the car-flipping example, imagine it takes you three months using the purchase method to save up the money you need to get your first car after four months (three months to save and one month to find and flip a car), your profit is $1,000. However, if you could balance transfer the money to yourself the first day you receive the promotion, you could have potentially flipped four cars and only needed to pay the fee for the original $2,000 once. After four months your profit is now $3,940! By using a balance transfer you could then pay off the card and take your new $3,940 profit to continue to do this without ever paying a fee again.

Buying Rentals with Credit Cards

As I stated before, 0% APR promotions are the main way to invest while using credit cards. One of the first investment opportunities that I used credit cards for was a chance to buy an already renovated and rented investment property—

which means the second I bought the property; I would begin collecting rent. The seller was offering a hard money loan for half of the property's value, but I would need to come up with the other half, roughly $25,000. It was not something I had in my bank account at the time! However, the seller did accept credit cards as payment. I had already been increasing the amount of credit cards I had, so I was ready to take advantage of this opportunity.

Since the credit cards I had been obtaining were new, they all gave me one to two years of 0% interest on any new purchases. These cards gave me about $18,000 of available credit. To come up with the other $7,000, I called the companies of the cards I already had and asked for a limit increase. I was able to get a total $4,000 increase from two different cards. Still $3,000 short, I put the last $3,000 on a credit card that did not have a 0% promotion available. I did, however, call and was able to obtain a 1.99% promotion for that card.

I ultimately bought the property with $25,000 on five different credit cards plus the hard money loan of $25,000.

The mortgage for the property was interest-only and just under $250 a month. Rent collected on the property was

$700 a month. I took the rent, paid the $250 mortgage, and used the rest to pay off the credit cards. I started first paying off the card that charged interest. From there I paid off the cards that only had a one-year promotion, followed by the two-year promotion cards.

I used more than just the rent to pay these cards off. If I had an extra dollar it went to paying off the cards. With discipline I paid off all the credit cards in the promotional time frame and only paid interest on the card that did not have the 0% promotion available. After two years of having the interest-only hard-money loan I was able to refinance the property into a more traditional loan. It makes me money every month, and if I never spend an extra dollar on it, it will be paid off less than twelve years from the time of writing this book.

I purchased another rental property by using balance transfers to take advantage of a 0%-interest promotion. I found a house that I thought was a good deal. It was run down, but it had potential. I ran the numbers and with purchase price, repairs, and carrying cost I felt it would make money. The home was listed at $78,000, but I negotiated it down to $76,500. I did not have that kind of cash in my account, so again I applied for a loan. Even though I got a hard-money loan, the lender would not finance 100% of the total cost. I needed to put down 10% plus pay all the fees of the loan out of pocket, which came to just under $14,000. I did not have that money in my bank account either. I had been working with credit cards for quite some time at this point and was ready to use them again. I had several cards that were offering me a 0% balance transfer promotion through access checks I received in the mail. Even though the rate was 0%, there was a 3% fee for using this promotion. This would cost me around $420 in fees. But even this $420 did not come out of my pocket. The fee was added to the balance of the card, so I was able to buy this property with literally no money out of pocket.

I then started to repair the home. The total cost of renovations and carrying cost was roughly $70,000 dollars. This was more than I had planned on because, unfortunately the home was found to have asbestos, plumbing, and wiring problems, which required a lot more work. What I had planned to be a relatively quick fix became a major project.

I did not have $70,000 to buy all the materials needed or to pay contractors for work I was required to get done professionally. So how did I pay for them? You guessed it—

with credit cards. I used Home Depot and Lowes credit cards to buy materials I needed, and I used contractors that accepted credit cards (or paid them with cash I was able to balance transfer to my own account). The total cost of the project turned out to be $145,000 dollars and took me ten months to complete. I could have sold the home for $175,000 at that time, leaving me with a profit of around $25,000 after the selling fees. That may not sound great for ten months' worth of work, but remember, this was done in my spare time.

Instead of selling it, I decided to refinance and turn it into a rental so I could earn money from it for years to come. I was able to refinance it for $125,000, allowing me to pay off my loan and most of the money on credit cards. That means that for work in my spare time and $20,000 on credit cards, I was again able to own a rental property. It is worth over $200,000 dollars now, which I can borrow against in the future, allowing me to purchase more rentals. None of this would have been possible if I was not able to balance transfer money from credit cards to cover the initial down payment and fees.

Neither of these two stories are home runs, but remember, becoming wealthy is a slow and steady process. A baseball team rarely wins a game by hitting only home runs. That is also how wealth is built. By adding one investment at a time.

CHAPTER FOUR: THE GIFT THAT KEEPS ON GIVING

The methods I've talked about thus far all help to put cash in your pocket. But there are even more ways that credit cards can help. They are truly the gift that keeps on giving!

These benefits won't directly help you save or earn money but are still fantastic tools not offered when using other methods of payment. Let's face it, once cash has left your hand, it's gone. The same is pretty much true for a check that has been cashed. Debit cards are a little better, but nothing is as safe as using a credit card.

Protection Against Fraud

Fraud protection is great. In fact, under the Fair Credit Billing Act it is law! Fraud protection prevents you from being responsible for any credit card charges that you didn't make.

If your credit card is ever stolen, you can kick up your heels and relax, because you won't have to pay anything that the thief purchased. This is one reason why some people refuse to carry cash. If someone steals your wallet and there's cash inside, you'll never get it back. If they steal your credit card, you may be out some time in phone calls, but your money is still all in the same place.

Some thieves don't even need your physical card, they just need the numbers. But, fraud protection saves you there too. If you browse through your charges and notice something suspect, just report the charge was not you and the money will come back to your account.

Many financial institutions even alert you if something is wrong! It can be annoying when you're traveling, but if you're sitting home watching television and get a text about a purchase in Iceland (unless you live in Iceland), you can stop it before it even starts.

Fraud protection is the best!!

Sometimes you run into someone that is trying to take advantage of you. Most of us know what it's like to be deceived. This usually happens in smaller ways but can be devastating when it happens on a larger scale. I was building a project from scratch, which meant I needed plans and someone else to build it. I began to interview contractors that could both create the plans and build the building. (Of course, I also wanted one that would accept credit cards for payment!) I found one but of course did my due diligence. I looked up the CCB number and it was in good standing, so I hired the contractor and paid around $4,500 to start the plans.

Then the stories started to come. It took longer and longer, and I never saw any work being done. I began to complain and pressed harder. I complained to the CCB board and found out that I was not the only one. It turns out that this particular contractor, and his father, had been making false contract companies for years. They would start a business, work on a few small projects, and then collect a lot of contracts by underbidding and overpromising. A lot of people took the bait. And then they would do it all over again with a new license, so they couldn't be tracked.

The good news is, I was a credit card user. Even though it had been months since I paid, I called the company and explained the situation. They documented it as fraud, and the money was back in my account the next day.

Unfortunately, many others lost money. The contractor conned about half a million dollars out of some people. Their insurance only covered $100,000, so most people they scammed were out of luck.

I was never more grateful that I had used a credit card.

Insurance Protection

Insurance against purchases is just what the name implies. You buy something and it gets lost, stolen, or broken and the credit card covers you. Not all credit cards offer this and terms vary quite a bit so will have to check with the credit card company to know what exactly is covered, but it can come in handing form time to time if you do have.

Travel Insurance

Again, the name says it all. When paying for travel expenses such as airfare, hotel, car rental, etc., if you use the right credit card you are covered against any issues.

This helps to take the stress off what should be a stress-free experience! Who hasn't had a lost bag, missing car rental, or snafu at a hotel? Last minute purchases in travel can get out of hand. This is just one more way a credit card has your back when other payment methods don't. Of course this too is not offered by all cards and terms do apply. So double check what is covered when planning your trip.

Ease of Records

This is one of my favorite perks. If I'm spending cash, I often wonder … where did it all go? A paycheck is great, but when it's depleted, sometimes you're not sure where. What did you buy that emptied your coffers so fast? I never seemed to document my expenses and I lose receipts even with the best of intentions.

Well, if you make all your purchases on credit cards you can look up any purchase you want. This is great for budgeting and seeing where you have areas of overspending. Keeping a budget and being aware of your spending is key to going from pauper to prince and credit cards cut out some record keeping naturally.

With credit cards, it's as simple as hitting print or downloading a file to see where you spent your money. This comes in very handy at tax time.

CHAPTER FIVE: IMPROVING YOUR CREDIT SCORE

With all of the different ways available to make and save money using credit cards, there are plenty to choose from that fit your personality and your management abilities. Finding the ones that work best for you is key to getting to your end goal.

But what if you can't even qualify for a credit card? In a country where the majority of people have "bad credit," how can you make this work?

There's no big secret. If you have a credit score so low you don't qualify for any credit card, you simply have to build your credit first. This can take some time and may seem daunting, but remember, "Rome wasn't built in a day." The great news is there are dozens of ways to improve your credit rating. By using as many methods as you can, you can find your credit score higher than you ever thought it might go. At some point, your credit will be so good that you won't even need to look for offers. Like moths to a flame, they will come to you without you ever needing to lift a finger.

Monitor Your Score

Credit scores drop much faster than they rise, so monitoring your credit is your first line of defense. Out of sight, out of mind works great for many things, but if your credit is out of mind then it could end up way off track. Monitoring your credit is relatively easy to do these days. There are many credit cards, banking apps, and websites that will all let you check you score for free. You just need to find one you like and use it. Also consider having alerts set up, where you can be notified of any concerns immediately by the financial institution.

An important aspect about monitoring your credit is knowing what to look for. The two main concerns are identity theft and errors. One way to recognize identity theft is if you see a request appear on your credit report that you did not approve. A new credit card for a pet food company being sent to a state where you do not live (yes that happened to me!) should be an immediate red flag. Identity theft is relatively easy to spot, but if you don't spot it quickly it can really set you back.

It is possible to monitor your credit for identity theft yourself and you can also take the steps to repair it yourself. Just know that it can be a very extensive process and require a lot of documentation!

Consequently, this is one of the few things I recommend having someone else do for you. There are plenty of companies that specialize in identity theft, or this area of monitoring can even be tacked on to some other service you already use. For example, I pay for a monitoring service through my tax accountant. When a company does the monitoring, they are more likely to catch identity theft long before it becomes a big issue.

Errors are often just as easy to spot. Errors are things like a debt you have already paid off showing up on your credit report or a late payment that wasn't actually late. In many of these cases, correcting the error is as simple as making a phone call to have your records updated. Errors are also something you can hire someone to monitor. Many of us have busy lives and calling creditors to have errors repaired can be time consuming if you have other things to do. They might also only accept calls during business hours, when most of us are also working! This makes hiring someone to correct the errors much less of a hassle than doing it yourself.

Errors can also often be fixed by the same companies that monitor identity theft, allowing you to kill two birds with one stone.

Errors seem to be common and will eventually get corrected on their own, but if you are having trouble qualifying for a card now, finding an error and having it corrected can easily push you over the hump.

> **Word to the Wise**
>
> When I was younger, I assumed that if I owed someone money, they would eventually call me to ask for it. I was attending college at the time and received GI bill benefits from my time in the service.
>
> They overpaid me $67 dollars, but I was unaware. They sent me a letter to inform me of the overpayment and my need to repay it. Unfortunately, I had finished school and moved before that letter was sent. I had not updated the school with my new address and thus never received the letter.
>
> Eventually I went to buy a car, only to realize my credit score was more than 100 points lower than I expected. I investigated, found out about the overpayment, and figured out the process to repay the money. The problem was that this debt had already been sent to collections ... not just any collections but the government's collections. When I tried to pay it to get if off my record, I was informed that it

> would come out of my next tax return—which was eight months away. Not only did I have an outstanding balance on my credit report, I couldn't even remove it for another eight months. After it was paid, it took seven years to come off my report entirely, affecting every loan I attempted to get. This put me almost a decade behind where I could have been had I been aware of my credit report.

Monitoring your credit score is much less time consuming than trying to repair your credit score. It is by far the easiest way to keep your credit stable and on an upward path.

Manage Your Credit Cards

In today's world it is rare for an American to have no credit card debt. Yet most people are unaware of the importance of managing their credit cards such that the debt does not negatively affect their credit score.

Set Up Automatic Payments

Since paying you bills on time is a great way to keep your credit score up, automatic payments are the best way to make sure that the chaos of life doesn't get in the way.

Even though most people only get paid once or twice a month, bills often span the range of the entire month. It's easy to have something get lost in the shuffle. I once was late to pay a bill because I went online and was distracted. I did everything except hit the submit button. Luckily the company could see the steps I had taken and cut me a break on a late charge, but I have not always been so lucky.

Even the most organized among us might still have something fall through the cracks now and then. While one or two late fees might not be a big deal, on the road to wealth they can become speed bumps and potholes that make the drive a lot less smooth. Setting up automatic payments can be the cruise control you need to make sure your financial ride isn't full of surprises.

There are a few other elements to check when setting up your automatic payments:

- Make sure there are no fees for setting up your automatic payments. Some companies charge a "convenience fee" for setting up autopay. To this day I have never thought of a "convenience fee" as very convenient.
- Check your payment date. Some companies allow you to choose the day and others require a specific date. If you can choose the date, make sure to set it before the payment is

due. If you can't choose the date, make sure it is a day when money will be available to pay the bill. Having an automatic payment set for the first of the month, when you get paid on the second, could be problematic.

- Double check your auto-pays from time to time. Every now and then companies change things, so this will help eliminate surprises.
- Set up the payment for the full amount, not the minimum payment. Most credit card companies set the payment to the minimum, but if you do not pay in full you will get interest charges.

Occasionally it won't make sense to put a particular bill on automatic payments, but for the most part this is a great way to eliminate human error as much as possible. It also helps cut down on the time you need to focus on keeping track of your finances. Even credit cards can't buy you more time.

Check Your Percentages

One thing to note is the percentage of debt on a card. Creditors look at both the dollar amount you owe and also the ratio of what you owe to what you can borrow. In other words, they check how much you owe on a card versus the limit of that card. If you owe $5,000 on a card with a $10,000 limit, you will have a higher credit score than if you owe $5,000 on a card with a $5,000 limit. The difference is the percentage you are in debt. With the first scenario you are only 50% in debt, but in the latter scenario you are 100% in debt. So, to raise your credit score you can either lower how much you owe on a card or call to raise the limit! You do have to qualify for a limit increase, but if it's available, this is a good tactic.

Note: the turning point seems to be 50%. After your accounts get below 50% owed, your score begins to climb. So, if you have the ability to adjust the debt between cards, it could help your score begin to travel in the desired direction.

Keep Your Cards Longer

Your credit score is also affected by how long you have your credit cards. Having a credit card for a long time shows loyalty, and companies are frequently willing to reward you for your loyalty by raising your credit score. Likewise, new accounts can lower your score for a time because they are unsure of what you are going to do with the new card. Are you going to keep the card for emergencies? Will you max out the card to buy a new living room set? Is it time to get that jet ski you always wanted?

You should carefully consider when to get rid of a card and when to get a new one. If you have a card that is old and it has been years since you've used it, as long as it is not costing you anything in fees, it is probably a good idea to keep it. Let the old card increase the average age of all your cards. Also, after you have built your credit up, don't sign up for credit cards that don't offer you a specific benefit. If it is not going to give you something for signing up, there is no reason to do so.

Take a Break from Applying

One final way to improve your credit score without paying something off is to stop applying for loans. Oftentimes when someone is looking for a loan, they apply for several to try to find the best deal they can get. Unfortunately, the more times you apply for credit in a given period of time, the lower your score will fall. If you happen to be on the cusp here, you can actually find yourself out of luck by trying to be a thrifty shopper. Every time you apply for credit an "inquiry" is added to your credit report. The more inquiries you have, the lower your score. The good news is that most will drop off after a six-month period. This means that you could potentially wait for six months to let all of the inquiries drop off, and that could raise your score enough to push you over the top.

If you use all of these money-free ways of improving your credit, your score could jump enough to allow you to start using the plastic gold mines I have outlined in this book. With every dollar you make there, you could pay off debt and see your score soaring off into the wild blue yonder.

Sign Up for a Secure Credit Card

If you're still struggling with your credit score, one of the most basic ways to increase it is to get a secure credit card, use it, and pay the bill.

A secured card is one on which you put a deposit. The way it works is you give a credit card company $200, and they give you a credit card that has a $200 limit. If you max out the card and don't pay the bill, the company keeps the deposit, and no money is lost.

These cards are the training wheels of the plastic world. Besides building your credit, these cards can help you build the discipline needed to master the spells of the plastic magic in this book. Secured cards can help you practice paying bills, keeping track of purchases, and only buying what you need, all within a manageable limit. In no time you will have mastered the small stuff and be ready to take off the training wheels.

Pay Your Bills and Negotiate

Another step that can improve your credit score is to pay your bills. It's no surprise that not paying your bills, or not paying them on time, will drop your credit score fast. This may seem like a no-brainer, but paying your bills is not always possible. Tragedy does sometimes strike, and if you are a fan of Murphy's Law, then you know it *will* strike. Sometimes the tragedy could be illness or job loss. Or it could be that as a teenager someone approved you for a credit card before your brain was fully developed, and the bling at the mall called your name, leaving you in debt long before you found this book. Whatever the reason, it is important that if you find yourself in a position where you cannot afford to pay all your bills, you get out of that position as quickly as possible. If your credit is not too far gone, you can use some of the strategies in this book to get back in the black. However, if your score is at rock bottom, you will have to take other steps to climb out of the hole.

The first thing you want to make sure you are doing is paying the bills you can. Ignoring them can turn a slide down a hill into plummet off a cliff. Keep up with the bills you can so when your life turns around you are not as far behind as you could have been.

Second, try to negotiate. A lot of creditors would rather have something than nothing. Many will work with you as best they can, so they get at least a small piece of what is owed. This can take many shapes.

Negotiate Interest-Only Payments

Interest-only payments allow you to only pay the interest each month, rather than both the interest and some of the principal. The benefit is that your monthly payment will be less, leaving you with money to help pay other debts. The downside to this is that the debt never gets any smaller. The best way to use this idea is to pay off another debt with the extra savings as fast as possible. Then when the first debt is paid off, take the payment that was going towards it and use it for the one that is currently interest-only.

For example, let's say you have two debts of $1,000 each, and you currently owe $200 monthly toward each debt. If both payments are 50% interest and 50% principal, then each month you are paying $100 in interest and $100 towards the actual debt.

However, say you only have $350 each month to pay these two bills. If you split the money 50/50 then you would be paying $175 toward each debt each month. Both companies start reporting that you are not paying your full bill, thus dropping your credit score and most likely adding late fees to your bill.

Let's say that you call one of the companies and convince them to let you pay interest only. Now you are committed to pay $100 to that company and $200 to the second company. If you were paying the original $400 a month, $200 to each bill, it would have taken you roughly 10 months to pay off both debts. If you are only paying the $175 each, and adding late fees, you may never pay them off. By convincing one creditor to accept interest only, you can take the same $350 you have, pay one creditor the $100 for the interest only, and pay $250 to the second creditor. That debt gets paid off in less than seven months and now you only have one debt remaining. You could pay the entire $350 to that creditor, paying off the debt in four additional months. This is a total of 11 months, which is only one month longer than the original plan of $200 per month toward each debt.

The immediate benefit to this is that both companies would now report that you are paying your bill in full and on time—thereby helping your credit. So even though you did not originally have enough money to pay both debts, with a little negotiating you can find yourself paying off debt at roughly the same pace.

Don't forget discipline though. Using the money you saved to pay off debt faster is a must if you plan on being debt free and building wealth in your life time.

Negotiate a Pay-Off

Another negotiation that can really help is a pay-off. This means that you convince a creditor to accept less than what is owed and then consider the debt paid in full. This works best with debt that has already been sent to collections. Collection agencies will buy debt from other companies that have gone past their normal collection time frames. When collection agencies buy debt, it is for pennies on the dollar. This helps the original debtor by stopping the unpaid debt from being a total loss, and it benefits collection agencies by giving them the freedom to settle the debt for less than what was originally owed, but more than they purchased it for. Often collection agencies purchase debt for ten to twenty percent of the original debt. Which means if you settle the debt for 50% of the original debt you could save by not needing to pay all the debt and the collection agencies makes 2.5 to 4 times their money.

As an example, let's say you purchase a TV for $1,000 on a credit card (which you would not have bought if you had read this book first unless you already had the money). After a few months of making payments, life happens, and you find yourself no longer able to make the payments. With interest, the debt climbs to $1,500 and then is sent to collections. You then find out that you are getting a tax return. Wisely you decide the use the money to eliminate debt. You call up the collection agency that bought your debt and see if they are willing to take $750 and call the debt paid in full. They say yes! You pay the $750 and you are no longer being reported as not making the monthly payment you couldn't afford.

Here only $750 is being erased; but there have been cases of people negotiating thousands of dollars off a debt. When negotiating with collections always start below half the amount of the entire debt. Better to start low and have them say "no" and it cost slightly more than to offer to pay more than they would have accepted if asked.

Negotiate a Reduction in Interest

Of course, it is better to negotiate before the debt goes to collections so you can preserve you credit score in the first place. They are less likely to reduce the amount owed, but there are other ways to negotiate into a situation you can afford. For instance ask for a reduction in interest charged.

For example, let's say you have a debt of $1,000 with a 10% monthly interest payment. That would cost $100 in interest every month. The payment is $200 with $100 in principal and $100 in interest. If you only had $180/month to pay toward this debt, and you talk the creditor into dropping the interest rate 2% so that you only need $180/month, then you could make your payment in full, have the creditor report you are paying in full, and still pay off the debt in the same amount of time.

Negotiate a Deferment

Many people ask for a deferment of either payments or interest. A deferment is a period of time where you do not make payments and/or are not charged interest. The benefit here can work two ways.

1. A deferment of payments can allow you to take the money you would have paid on one debt and put it toward a second debt. If in doing this you could get the second debt paid off, it would free up the money you are using for that debt to pay the first debt at the end of the deferment.
2. In the case of deferred interest, having no interest charged leaves your entire payment going to principal, thereby lowering the amount you owe faster so when the deferment ends you will be charged less in interest because there is less debt to be charged interest on.

> **The Negotiation Table**
>
> My sister and her husband found themselves in debt when they made a necessary move from one town to another. As a tattoo artist, she lost a lot of her client base and walk-in

traffic. Like most people that lose a job, this large loss of income left them turning to the credit cards they already had for basic needs like food. After about a year my sister was back on her feet, unfortunately, the damage had already been done. She had over $10,000 of debt that went to collections. Since she was unable to manage the monthly payments, her credit score dropped so low there was no hope of her getting a loan to pull her out.

What saved her? Credit cards of course. In this case, the credit cards that saved her belonged to me. I used a balance transfer promotion from one of my credit cards to get her $9,000 cash to pay off her debt. We agreed that she could use the money as long as she covered all fees and payments. This she could do because she made enough money from work with all her new clients, even though her credit was too low to get a credit card herself.

Armed with cash, we called her debtors and began to negotiate. We always started with less than half of the amount owed. Most of it was interest after all. After a few hours she was able to negotiate $11,000 of debt down to $6,373 which she paid off that day with the money from my cards balance transfer. She took the remainder of the original $9,000 to pay off some of her smaller debts that had not yet gone to collections. This not only saved her $4,627, but also started her credit repair on a steep upward path.

Become an Authorized User

One of the easiest ways to improve your credit score is by becoming an authorized user on a credit card account that is already in good standing.

How do you do this? Ask a relative or friend if they have a credit card in good standing and see if they will add you to their account.

This is especially beneficial if you can't qualify for your own card, as your credit card will improve being tied to this other card. When the owner of the card pays the bill, your credit will report that you have an account that is being paid on time. This then raises your credit score. The credit card company allows this and benefits because they have more people responsible to pay the debt.

Keep in mind that you shouldn't be using this card! As soon as you get it, cut up your copy, sit back, and watch your credit score climb.

Of course, this method does require that you know someone who is willing to let you on to their account. Not all of us have someone willing to do so, but if you do, this is a great way to get started.

Consider Ways to Earn More or Spend Less

The last thing that can really help out when you find yourself in a monthly deficit is to earn more money. Now I know some of you are saying, "duh," but hear me out. Discipline can be used for more than *not* doing something. It can also be critical in getting you to *do* extra. No one expects someone to be a body builder without doing extra work—building wealth is no less of a time commitment than sculpting a Mr. Universe-worthy body. However, unlike sculpting the perfect body, wealth can eventually accumulate without you needing to put much effort in. And even better, wealth grows with age instead of fading.

Becoming rich can often be unglamorous and require a lot of extra work. I certainly don't have a face for the movie screen. That is why I chose working hard as my method of earning more money. Just a few extra hours a week can make a big difference in how much money you bring home. You could also do a one-time thing to help. Maybe it is time for that garage sale you have been considering for years. If you could make money by cleaning out the clutter, and then take that money to pay off debt, you would find it much easier to breathe when the first of the month rolls around.

Don't want to work more? Perhaps you can try spending less. Cancel cable and stick to Netflix. Let movie night be with Redbox instead of a trip to the theater. Cook food instead of getting it delivered by Door Dash.

Whatever you do, spending the extra effort to come up with just a little extra cash can really help you climb out of the credit hole. Once your credit score is high enough, you can use the credit cards themselves to reach new financial heights. Remember, the difference between ordinary and extraordinary is *extra*.

CHAPTER SIX: BUILDING WEALTH AND INVESTING FOR GROWTH

This is a book about the incredible uses of credit cards, but I do feel we need to quickly chat about building wealth with this newfound money! There are so many things to invest in, and I am not going to go into specifics here because there are hundreds of books on that topic. What I want to do is give you a few key notes as you begin to decide where you want to grow your wealth.

Build Your Wealth

Most people haven't considered that building wealth could start by getting more credit cards. But it's not the *what* that builds wealth but the *how* I want to talk about. There are a lot of misconceptions about building wealth, and I would like to dispel some of them.

Wealth tends to come to people in three ways:

1. They are born into it.
2. They luck into it.
3. They work their way into it.

The common thread with the first two methods of gaining wealth is speed and ease. But being born in to wealth does not guarantee you keep it and your luck can run out, leaving these two ways of obtaining wealth as shaky foundations at best. While the first two ways may seem great, the truth is that most wealthy people build their wealth over a long period of time through the third method: lots of work and discipline.

Yes, some people might have a slight edge, but the truth is that hard work and discipline is really what is needed to rise to level of stardom. Athletes usually practice for years before they make it to the big leagues. Musicians also do this. In fact, one of the most famous groups of all time, The Beatles, played music day in and day out at clubs before they made it big.

It is not a rocket ride to wealth, but rather a slow steady climb up a mountain of work with a promise of an amazing view at the top. Along the journey comes a great sense of accomplishment and the ability to share your story and your formula for success with future generations.

With that in mind, let's talk about the surest way to build wealth. The hard work starts by getting yourself on the correct track. If you have made a habit of spending money you don't have and/or spending every dollar you make on things that don't make you money (e.g., eating out, attending movies, buying things) then the first thing to do is STOP.

Take an inventory of what you make and what you spend. Yes, this is called a budget. A budget lets you take stock on your life right now. It can also show you where you are headed financially. If you find you spend more than you make, then you can take steps to fix it. Call people and companies to whom you owe money and work something out. If your credit is good, use some of the ways in this book to make and save money to catch up. If your credit is not good, dig deep and find some extra ways to make a little more money. This may take some time, but it needs to be done. You can't build a strong foundation on a sink hole.

> **The Stack**
>
> As of the writing of this book, I currently have twenty-two credit cards with over $150,000 of available credit. I only owe money on three of these cards, and one of those is the card I use for groceries. I have used these cards for anything from flipping houses and buying rentals, to remodeling bathrooms without paying interest. I also receive between $5,000 to $10,000 every year in cash as rewards from them. Investments I have bought using credit cards net me more

than $1,000 a month that I don't have to work for, and I am still adding to my investment portfolio.

At this point, no matter what I decide to invest in I know I can have the funds available in just a few days if not instantly. I still take advantage of promotions that come my way, and always look for new ways to benefit from credit cards. I will also continue to increase the size of my stack. As it grows, so too, do my possibilities.

Mind Your Own Business

Robert Kiyosaki said it best in his book *Rich Dad Poor Dad* (a book I highly recommend) when he said, "mind your own business." What he meant by this is that you need to build a business for yourself and not just work for someone else your whole life. But you can also take this to mean "stick to what you do best."

My sister has been a tattoo artist for years. She worked for tattoo shop owners most of her career, sometimes giving them half of her income to have a workspace in their shop. After several conversations with me about building wealth, she decided to open her own shop. She realized that by owning her own shop she would get to keep everything she made, plus she could make money by renting out space to other artists. She gets to set the rules and she works less hours but brings home more money! By sticking to what you already know, you can find plenty of opportunities without having to reinvent the wheel.

Educate Yourself

Now that you've taken inventory and started to focus, it's time to educate yourself. Explore several different fields in which you feel you can make some money. Or if you have a great idea, learn what it would take to make it work. Read books, study what people have done in the past that worked and try your best to find someone with personal experience. This step is needed because it is what will let you take risk without losing everything on one bad deal. There will always be *some* risk. However, just as you would not risk your life by jumping out of a plane without a parachute, you should not risk your financial life without knowing what can go wrong and having a backup plan.

A lot of people say they *invest* in the stock market, but I would say many of them *gamble* in the stock market.

What's the difference? Knowledge.

The people who successfully play the stock market spend time at it. They read articles daily, they keep up on companies and news that can impact their investments, and they take steps to keep their money safe. They are educated and continually develop their knowledge. This keeps them in the game long term. If you are about to risk your hard-earned money, wouldn't you want to know about the companies and products you are spending it on? Yet plenty of people will risk hundreds, if not thousands, of dollars on a whim or on someone's passing comment.

> **Trading Currencies**
>
> I once decided I would like to try trading in the foreign exchange. This is merely trading money from one currency to another, trying to make money by having the value of a currency rise or fall in comparison to the currency you would like to have more of. I studied for six months before I used real money. I read over a dozen books, bought two different learning programs, and opened a paper (non-real money) account. I traded in my paper account for several months and then tried my hand at real money. After trading real money for six months, I broke even and decided it was time to move on. I recognized that people who make a living by trading in this market spend a lot of time on a regular basis to do so. They read articles, kept up on current events, and studied charts daily. I *could* do that, but decided it was not for me. Even though I did not make money in the

> foreign exchange, the experience taught me a lot, and gave me valuable experience I can still use in other ways to help me build wealth.

Education comes in many ways. You can read up on a subject or even take classes on investing. One of the best moves you can make is to find someone who already invests successfully in the field you are interested in and learn from them. Just as martial arts students are taught by masters that have spent years perfecting their craft, those who want to learn about investing would be wise to learn from those who are masters at it. There is no substitute for actual experience.

While I do recommend education on investing, I do not necessarily recommend seminars and the like. Feel free to go to as many free ones as you like but be selective about the ones that ask you to pay to attend. Also remember, the people leading the seminars are salesmen—not investors. They are well trained and know how to get people emotionally involved to increase the chances of selling their product.

Do Your Homework

Always make sure to do your homework. Some opportunities come and go quickly. This gives people a sense of needing to strike while the iron is hot. While this can be true, it is more important to investigate the deal before you spend your money. It does you no good to buy a $100,000 house for $50,000 if there is a $60,000 lien that you were unaware of. You won't be able to eliminate all risk of investing, but by doing your homework you can minimize the risk as much as possible. Not every deal will be a success, but the key is to have more successes than failures and to learn as much as possible from the failures. If in taking the time to investigate a deal you end up losing it to someone else, have no fear. Another deal will come along.

Make Money ... Don't Lose It!

It is only an investment if it makes you money. This may seem like stating the obvious, but very often people will buy something only to discover that the deal costs them money. If you want to buy a house with the intention of turning it into a rental, you need to do your homework to make sure the rent you charge covers all the expenses. Let's say, however, you fail to take into consider the homeowner's association fees and now you find yourself collecting $1,000 of rent but having $1,100 of expenses every month. This is not an investment—investments make money, not lose it.

Build Your Buffer Zones

You absolutely want to build in a buffer zone in case something goes wrong. In the case of a rental property, you want to have a couple of months of mortgage payments in the bank in case you don't have a renter during that period. If you can't do that, then this investment might not be the best option for you. A lot of people find themselves out of the investment game because they failed to account for the unexpected. Life happens. Even if you don't know what problems might arise, you need to plan for them. A winner can become a loser very fast when an unexpected event comes up without a backup plan.

Use Those Credit Cards!

I've taught you many things in the previous chapters. But one way you can really move mountains is with limit increases.

Limit increases can be great for three things: getting more debt on 0% interest, increasing your credit score (as we discussed above), and having more money for investing.

You can get a limit increase by simply picking up the phone for an existing credit card and asking the financial institution if you can raise the limit. You do have to qualify for the increase, but you can usually ask for one without it hurting your credit score.

Using a limit increase to pay off debt is a simple concept to implement. If you can transfer a debt with a higher rate to a card offering you a 0% promotion, then you are ultimately paying less interest on the debt overall and that is all money in your pocket.

But, let's talk about using limit increases for investing. Let's say you did your research and are ready to start your own business by purchasing a food truck. You need to spend about $5,000 on the truck and another $10,000 on supplies. Unfortunately, between your savings and what you can use on 0% interest promotions you only have $5,000.

It doesn't make much since to buy the truck without supplies because then you would be paying on a debt that is not making you money. Remember, if it is not making you money, it is not an investment. Instead of applying for a new credit card, consider asking your existing institution to increase your limit. If they do, you're ready to get started!

This is a strategy I have implemented many times to fill in the gap of buying or repairing one of my rental properties. It allows me to start the cashflow now rather than later. And if it is all done on 0% interest promotions, there is no additional cost!

Face Your Obstacles

You will run into obstacles. These will include fear, being told your plan won't work, or even falling into the trap of constantly learning and never doing.

You will make mistakes. Mistakes, after all, are a part of life. That is why we make backup plans. As the saying goes, you can't make an omelet without breaking a few eggs.

You will run into naysayers. Do not let them talk you out of your dreams. As a teenager, I stopped with a friend at a gas station to fill up. I was talking to my friend about ideas I had to retire early and become wealthy. The store attendant, a middle aged women missing several teeth, told me that would never happen, and I was dreaming. When I tried to explain my plan, she looked at me, and through her toothless smile she said, "Can you say, dream on?" I did dream on, and now I am well on my way to becoming wealthy and making my dreams come true. But it all started with my trying in the first place.

You will want to quit. Don't. You've heard the saying, "If at first you don't succeed, try, try again." The first home I ever flipped was relatively easy. I tried it and it worked out, but I only made $2,500 when it was all said and done. Definitely not the big numbers most people hope for! I lost $7,000 on the second home I flipped. This after spending a whole year putting in labor at night after doing my day job to cover my family's expenses. I could have stopped there and said, "I have tried flipping houses and it doesn't work." The truth is, though, that it can work. I knew other people had done it, which meant I could too.

The third house I flipped I made $5,000. It took me around a year to do, but I was back in the black. This may seem disheartening to spend several years working extra-long hours to earn what equates to only a few hundred dollars. However, along the way I learned a lot. I also decided I would focus on rentals instead of flipping homes. I now own several income producing properties.

You just have to keep going. As I said before, becoming wealthy is like climbing a mountain. It will be step by step, reach by reach. You may even fall a few, if not several, times. And like climbing a mountain, falling is terrifying, even when you know your safety measures will keep you unharmed. But you can't make it to the top if you don't keep going and you won't be wealthy if you quit early.

Explore a Possibility

For those of you who still aren't sure where to start, I want to offer a possible scenario of a pathway to becoming wealthy.

An eighteen-year-old graduates high school and decides to get a job. After two years of working the job, she now makes enough money to qualify for a loan to buy a home. (If she had read this book, she would also have used credit cards to make a few grand!) She buys her first home at 20 years old. Of course, she does not buy a dream home, but a fixer-upper. She spends a year living there while she fixes it up little by little after work. She does this by using credit cards (with a 0% rate for one to two years) to buy all the necessary materials and tools. Then she refinances it—because it is now worth more after all her hard work—and pays off the credit cards before the time comes to pay a higher interest rate.

Now that she has finished her upgrades, she finds someone willing to rent it for more than the total monthly expenses. She cannot qualify for two homes so she moves into an apartment until she can claim the first home as a rental on her taxes, showing the home as income instead of debt.

She's now 22 and wants to apply for another fixer upper. She's been saving the extra rental income and uses it as extra money down on the second home, so her loan isn't as large. Therefore, she makes more money by paying less interest. She again uses credit cards to buy materials, only this time it costs less as she already owns the tools from the first home.

If she was to repeat this process once every two years, by the time she turns 40, she will own ten rental properties. Let's assume that she makes $100 per property on average. That means at forty years of age she makes $1,000 a month without her needing to go to a job to get it. Not yet wealth but a very nice step in that direction.

Now let's say she continues this till she is fifty years old. She will now have 15 properties making $1,500 a month. And since it's been 30 years, the first home she bought should be paid off. Let's say the mortgage on that home was $1,000. Now she is making $2,500 dollars a month, after taxes and expenses, in residual income.

If no other changes occur, she will continue to pay off another mortgage every two years for the next thirty years.

Taking it a step farther, let's say she gets faster at fixing up houses and can buy them more frequently. From age 24–40 she buys ten homes instead of eight! And of course, the housing market has increased in 30 years, and she can borrow against that value to invest elsewhere.

And, what if the interest rate for mortgages drops? Then she can refinance and pay less every month even though the rent collected would stay constant. This means more money in her pocket each month. She is able to do it all because she could use credit cards to get the money for repairs, and every time she refinances a home to turn it into a rental, the credit cards get paid off and she never has to pay interest.

I can hear you naysayers: What if the market goes down? Even if the market goes down, rent doesn't. What about cost-of-living increases? Rent goes up from time to time to cover this. What if I am already forty—what am I supposed to do? Work at it from age forty to fifty and have five rentals to help cover retirement.

There are a thousand ways to tear this scenario apart and a thousand reasons not to take action. If you don't do something different, your life won't change. But what if you do take action? How might your life change? Remember, you don't have to get there with rentals. Choose another place to invest, just do it in a way that makes your dreams come true. Life is short. Shoot for the moon. That way even if you miss you might hit a few stars.

Conclusion

On the road to wealth, home runs can be very rare. But the end goal does not have to be reached quickly. Just as the tortoise beat the hare, you too can win the race by slow, steady progress. You will still be wealthy at the finish line. Looking for home runs every time might leave you feeling discouraged and cause you to quit the game too early. It is the doubles, singles and even bunts that slowly add to the score to bring victory. But you can't win if you never step up to the plate.

www.ingramcontent.com/pod-product-compliance
Lightning Source LLC
Chambersburg PA
CBHW022106170526
45157CB00004B/1499